GOD KNEW YOU WOULD CHOOSE HIM

SO HE CHOSE YOU

JOSHUA STRADER

Paperback ISBN: 978-0-578-88800-2

Straderministries.org

CONTENTS

CHAPTER 1

THE END FROM THE BEGINNING - GOD KNEW YOU WOULD CHOOSE HIM

2 Thessalonians 2:13 KJV But we are bound to give thanks always to God for you, brethren beloved of the lord, because God hath from the beginning chosen you to salvation through sanctification of the spirit and belief of the truth.

To every person that has ever become a child of God through being born again and accepting Christ's free gift of salvation and every person who ever will, God knew you would be his because he knew the end from the beginning. He knew you would choose Christ. The purpose of this book is to reveal to you that God has known and cherished each and every one of his children long before they got here and the world was made, and he loved them then. If you have not yet accepted Christ as your savior, you can become God's child by believing on him and accepting his gift of salvation.

The reason you can never be separated from the love of God is because you have been in it all along. As long as God has been love, and that's forever, he has known you and loved you. When you were conceived in your mother's womb is not the first time you were conceived. You were first conceived in the imagination and heart of God who is love long ago. And he knew you, he knew what your name would be, he knew the day you would believe on Christ, and he knew you would be his and he justified you then, based on that foreknowledge.

Psalm 139:16 NASB Your eyes have seen my formless substance; and in your book were written all the days that were ordained for me, when as yet there was not one of them.

Psalm 139:16 NLT You saw me before I was born. Every day of my life was recorded in your book. Every moment was laid out before a single day had passed.

Think about that for a second. He saw you before you were born. But how far before? According to other passages of scripture, before the foundation of the world. God knew me before the world existed? Yes! He did. *"In your book were written all the days that were ordained for me"* and *"every day of my life was recorded in your book"* shows us that in his foreknowledge God knows every choice we would make, and our days have been written before we got here. There are more scriptures which tell us the same thing. I am not saying that God ordained the bad or negative things that happen to us. What I'm saying is that he saw everything that would happen beforehand whether it was good or bad and has it written down. God does not wish for any of his children to be defeated, struggle through life, be plagued by sickness or disease, or bound by addictions or poverty. We know this because the word of God tells us that Jesus came to redeem us from those things and from the curse of the law.

Ecclesiastes 1:9-10 KJV The thing that hath been, it is that which shall be; and that which is done is that which shall be done: and there is no new thing under the sun. Is there anything whereof it may be said, see, this is new? It hath been of old time which was before us.

Ecclesiastes 3:15 KJV That which hath been is now; and that which is to be hath already been; and God requireth that which is past.

These are some very powerful statements in scripture. "The thing that has been is what shall be, That which is done is that which shall be done, Everything that happens hath been of old time which was before us, That which is going to happen hath already been."

Let's look at the Hebrew definitions to see what God's word is telling us.

In verse 10 of Ecclesiastes chapter 1, *"it hath been already"* - [H3528 kebar; already, long ago, a great while]

"of old time" - [H5769 o-lawm; everlasting, perpetual, ancient, eternal]

"which was before us" - [H6440 paw-neem';face, in front of, formerly, before]

Verse 15 of Ecclesiastes chapter 3, *"and that which is to be hath already been"* [H3528 kebar; already, long ago, a great while]

As you can see, there is nothing God doesn't already know. This is even down to the choices people make. There is nothing that will ever happen that will come as a surprise to him. Doesn't it feel good to know that your father already knows everything. Things may come as a surprise to us, but they don't come as a surprise to God. What I want us to see from these scriptures is that God has all wisdom and there is nothing that any person can do that he didn't already know about in the beginning before anything was made. He's that wise and has that much knowledge. And the Holy spirit deemed it worthy of being in the scriptures.

Isaiah 46:10 KJV Declaring the end from the beginning, and from ancient times the things that are not yet done, saying, My counsel shall stand, and I will do all my pleasure.

I want you to think about those words, *"Declaring the end from the beginning."* The beginning of what? From the beginning of all things. From the beginning of all things, God has already *"declared"* what the end will be.

[declared; H5046 hebrew-nagad, to tell, to make known, announce, publish].

God says here he publishes or makes known what the end will be from the very beginning, and from ancient times, the thing which is not yet done.

[ancient times, H6924 Keh-dem, that which is before, ancient time, afore time]

This shows us his omniscience (the state of knowing everything) as do many other passages. He is establishing the fact that he knows all things that will ever happen ahead of time, and that what he has seen happening is what will inevitably take place, even with everyone's freewill factored into the equation. Some people think that this means God predestined everything that happens even the evil in the world and that's not what it means. He didn't predestine the evil in the world, but he did know about it. And he did know what every person would do throughout history, including all those who would be his children, and those he saw accepting Christ he called, justified, and glorified. The word of God said those things in the past tense as we will see in a moment.

Acts 15:18 KJV known unto God are all his works from the beginning of the world.

What about Free will? Doesn't the scripture teach we have a free will?

Yes! It does! You and I do have a free will to make choices. We make decisions every day at home, on the job. Choices and the ability to choose is part of our everyday life. We have the power to choose where we are going to eat dinner on a particular evening, where we want to travel for vacation and many other things such as which route we want to take to the grocery store. It's your choice whether you do or don't do something, including whether you believe Jesus is the son of God and became sin in your place, so you don't have to suffer the consequence of eternal separation from him. It's your choice, you choose what you do and say, and what you believe! We definitely have free will.

You can't make a choice God didn't know about before the world was made

We most definitely have the power of choice, aka freewill. However, I want you to hear me when I tell you this. Even though you have a freewill, you do not have the power to exercise it outside of the foreknowledge of God. In other words, you cannot make any choice good or bad, that he didn't know about before the creation of the world. Because of his omniscience, there is nothing we can do in this life that he hasn't already seen beforehand. Again, just because God already saw every decision that was made, that doesn't mean he condoned every decision that was made. There's a big difference.

We do not have the ability to make a decision that God didn't know we would make before he made the world. I will show you later that the apostle Paul also believed this from things he wrote in his epistle to the romans.

God didn't choose some to go to heaven and some to go to hell

What this means when it comes to the salvation of individuals is this - God did not choose some to go to hell and some to go to heaven. Quite the opposite. He gave each of us the power of choice. The power to choose life or death, to believe on his son Jesus or to reject him. But at the same time, because he is God and is all knowing, he cannot help but know every choice an individual will ever make and the outcome or fate of that person even though those individuals do have a free will while living on the earth.

He knew you, loved you, will keep loving you, and made you special

He knows the end from the beginning is not just a broad statement that only applies to certain things like nations. It applies to everything. He knew you; he knew every breakthrough you would receive. He knew what your name would be, what your calling would be. He knew if you would love cats, and what kind of food would be your favorite. He made you unique and special. He knew you before you got here, he knew you would be his. God the father already knew personally and intimately each individual that would ever be his through the ages of time and he decided then at that time that those that would be his children would be blameless in his sight through the price that Jesus would pay on their behalf. He knew you, he loved you, and he will keep on loving you. You can never be separated from his love because you are his child. In the next chapter we will see in greater detail of what this means for those that he foresaw believing on Jesus.

CHAPTER 2

BEFORE THE FOUNDATION OF THE WORLD

Ephesians 1:4-5 KJV According as He hath chosen us in him before the foundation of the world, that we should be holy and without blame before him in love: Having predestinated us unto the adoption of children by Jesus Christ to himself, according to the good pleasure of his will.

We discussed how great the foreknowledge of God is. And we saw how God, who declares the end from the beginning and all things in between, already knows every choice that would be made with anyone's freewill while on earth. One choice that he saw ahead was that every person would have the power to choose whether they believed on Jesus or not. And that leads us into the next thing which is important for you to know. And it is this, God saw every single person that would ever believe on Jesus before he even made the world and before the fall of man. And every person that he fore-knew or saw believing beforehand, he also called, justified and glorified according to Romans 8:29-30 which we will take a look at in a moment.

But first let's look at the text in *Ephesians 1:4-5 According as he hath chosen us in him before the foundation of the world, that we should be holy and without blame before him in love...*

The first thing I want us to see in this is that *"he hath chosen us in him"*

This is letting us know that God decided that every person that would believe on Jesus while living on the earth would be chosen by him. He saw ahead of time that they would be believers and chose them to be *"in him."*

The second thing I'd like us to see is that he has chosen *"that we should be holy and without blame before him"*

Verse 5 *Having predestinated us* [G4309 proorizo; to predetermine, decide beforehand, ordain] *unto the adoption of children by Jesus Christ to himself; according to the good pleasure of his will.*

The word predestinated only has one meaning in the Greek; to predetermine/decide beforehand.

I'd also like you to see that the choice that those who would believe on Jesus while on the earth would be innocent and blameless in his sight was also made *"before the foundation of the world."* And that it was his *"good pleasure"* to do so. Praise God for the riches of his mercy.

What does this mean? God "proorizo" or decided beforehand that all who would ever believe on his son would be adopted by him and be blameless in his sight because of the price that Jesus would pay in their place. He decided beforehand that we would be without blame before him. I'd like us to see the power of this decision he made back then. The price that

Jesus paid was more than enough. It is finished and the Holy wrath of God against all lawlessness has been completely satisfied in the body of the Lord Jesus Christ for the believer. This doesn't mean there's no chastisement because the word of God let's us know that he chastens whom he loves. But his chastening is not the same thing as his judgment that comes upon those who reject Christ. He chastens us in love not in wrath.

There will be judgments poured out on the earth preceding the second coming of Christ that are mentioned in the book of Revelation, but those judgments are for the ungodly and the world, not the believer. All sin for the believer was absorbed into the body of the precious lord as he hung upon the cross. He became sin for us and in our place. If anyone ever asks me, "how could I be righteous in the sight of God if I haven't done any righteous deeds?" my response is "how did Jesus become sin when he never did any sin?" Friends it is a work of the spirit. God, in his all-knowing state, knew all that would ever be his by believing on Christ through an act of their freewill and pre-decided they would be justified in his sight because the sacrifice was enough, the price was paid in full at calvary. No debt was left. Their entire sin debt washed away with the blood of the innocent lamb slain from the foundation of the world. Hallelujah!

Let's look at *Romans 8:29-30 KJV For whom he did foreknow, he also did predestinate to be conformed to the image of his Son, that he might be the firstborn among many brethren. Moreover whom he did predestinate, them he also called: and whom he called, them he also justified: and whom he justified, them he also glorified.*

For whom he did foreknow [G4267 proginosko; to have knowledge beforehand, to foreknow, predestinate, foresee]

he also did predestinate [G4309 proorizo; to predetermine, decide beforehand]

to be conformed to the image of his son, that he might be the firstborn among many brethren.

Moreover whom he did predestinate [G4309 proorizo; to predetermine, decide beforehand]

them he also called [G2564 kaleo; to call, invite]

and whom he called, them he also justified [G1344 dikaioo; to render righteous, to pronounce one to be just, to show or regard as just or innocent]

and whom he justified, them he also glorified.

I want you to notice that all these things are written in the past tense, as if they have already happened. This was done to indicate to us that God see's it this way because he saw the end from the beginning before the world began. Friend, it is Gods will for you to know how saved you are and how Jesus has made you his righteousness. There is so much love and grace and goodness that he can't wait to lavish on you. But first it is needful for you to see how justified you are. God has set things up this way. It isn't mine or your plan, it's his and it's perfect. This is not a confusing subject. It is a blessed truth that is revealed throughout many pages of the bible. Any person that has ever believed or will ever believe, he knew them from the beginning.

Another example of this can be found in *Jeremiah 1:5 KJV Before I formed thee in the belly, I knew thee.*

If you are a believer, he knew you from the beginning. In fact, because he knows the end from the beginning, anyone who will ever be born again through faith in Christ was already known by God in the beginning. God the father knows every single individual that has ever put faith in Christ or will put faith in Christ and he has already chosen or decided that they would be blameless in his sight. And any person that God will ever know he already knew from the beginning. To deny this would be to deny his omniscience. A very well-known scripture also states the same thing but on the negative side of things. In Matthew 7:23 Jesus told certain individuals, "Depart from me ye that work iniquity, I *never knew* you." This is a clear reference to the fact that he never knew them from the beginning. For if he had known them, it would have been a lie for him to tell them he never knew them. I want to ask you a question. If Jesus ever does know a person, doesn't that mean he has known them from the beginning? Of course, it does. Therefore, for Jesus to tell an individual that he never *knew them*, he must be speaking of the fact that he never knew them from the start.

In John 10:27 Jesus said, "My sheep hear my voice, and *I know them*, and they follow me." Notice that Jesus said he knows his sheep. So, it would be impossible for him to ever tell one of them that he never knew them. If you have been born again, you are one of his sheep, and he said he knows you. Therefore, he can never tell you, "I never knew you" because that would be a lie and Jesus doesn't lie. This scripture has been used to preach born again people into the fear of being condemned by God, but Jesus said he knows his sheep and it would be a lie for him to ever tell one of them he never knew them. He was referring to people that never had been born again in the first place. They used his name to prophesy or cast out demons, but they were not born again.

Does this mean that he chose them to go to hell? No, it simply means that he knew from the beginning whether or not they would believe on him.

If you don't believe that God knew every single individual that would ever be his through a choice of their own freewill, then you don't yet understand how all-knowing he is. Let this revelation sink in and produce rest for your soul. You are his because he fore-saw and knew you would accept him in this life, and you have received *eternal Life.*

CHAPTER 3

ETERNAL LIFE

John 10:28 I give unto them eternal life, and they shall never perish...

This is a wonderful statement from the lips of the savior. We're going to take a look at the surrounding verses and its context in a moment, but before we do, I'd like us to take a look at the meaning of the word eternal.

Eternal [G166 ahee-o-nee-os, Thayer definition: 1. Without beginning and end, that which always has been and always will be, 2. Without beginning, 3. Without end, never to cease]

Notice that two of the three definitions of the word translated into the English word eternal are "without beginning." It's important for us to understand that when the word eternal is used here it literally means without beginning or end, not just without end. It is important that we understand this when reading and studying the scriptures that speak of eternal life. The life that we have in Christ has always been and always will be, and it has always been and always will be eternal. It existed in him before the foundation of the world. It's without beginning because God already knew us before we got here, he knew we would be his, and we existed in his imagination and heart in eternity past.

We were in him before anything was made because God in his omniscience, already knew all that would ever be his through the ages of time. This must be the case, or he wouldn't be God. He knew them. He knew the day they would believe on Christ, down to the very minute. He knew every single person that would ever be his and that made them his in his sight before they were ever conceived. He's that wise and that all-knowing that no one can ever make a choice he didn't know beforehand. Aren't you glad he knows you?

In *John 10:24-29 Then came the Jews round about him, and said unto him, How long dost thou make us to doubt? If thou be the Christ, tell us plainly. Jesus answered them, I told you and you believed not: the works that I do in my Father's name, they bear witness of me. But ye believe not because ye are not of my sheep, as I said unto you. My sheep hear my voice, and I know them, and they follow me: And I give unto them eternal life; and they shall never perish, neither shall any man pluck them out of my hand. My Father, which gave them me, is greater than all; and no man is able to pluck them out of my father's hand.*

Let's examine the context of these verses. It begins with the Jews asking Jesus if he is the Christ. And Jesus began to answer their question by saying he had already told them, and they didn't believe. He continues and tells them that the reason that they did not believe and many of them would not believe on him is because they were not his sheep. He is saying that if they were his sheep they would believe. I don't want us to miss the insight that we can gain from these beautiful passages of scripture. After telling them *"Ye believe not because ye are not of my sheep"* he proceeds to tell them that his sheep do hear his voice, *"My sheep hear my voice."*

What I'd like us to see is that Jesus was confident about this. He really believed that his sheep would hear his voice. He also say's *"and I know them, and they follow me."* Jesus firmly believed that his sheep would hear his voice and follow him. Those that the father foreknew in other words.

The statement *"and I know them"* is referring to individuals that believed on him and those that would in the future because as we saw, God already knows all who are going to accept Christ, even before they do.

He continues to say that he gives his sheep *"eternal"* life, which as we saw means life without beginning or end.

and that *"they shall never perish"* [G622 apollumi; Thayer 1. To destroy, abolish, kill, render useless, 2. to lose]

He said those that believe on him shall never perish or be destroyed, cut off, rendered useless or lost. That's awesome!

Then he continues to tell them, *"Neither shall any man pluck them out of my hand."* Remembering that the context of these passages is believing or not believing on Jesus, this is without doubt a strong emphasis of the fact that his sheep will always be his.

Also notice that he continues to emphasize the point and goes on to say, *"My Father which gave them me is greater than all and no man is able to pluck them out of my father's hand."*

What did he mean by the word pluck?

Pluck G726 harpazo; to seize, claim for oneself, to snatch away, to take.

No man is able to pluck, seize, snatch away or take us out of his hand.

Jesus also said all those the father gives to him will come to him. In *John 6:36-37 But I said unto you, that ye also have seen me, and believe not. All that the father giveth me shall come to me; and he that cometh to me I will in no wise cast out.*

I'd like us to notice that when he made the statement *"All that the father giveth me shall come to me"* that this further validates the fact that Jesus believed his sheep would definitely hear his voice, believe on him, and follow him. He wouldn't have said it if he didn't. Jesus believed that "All" that the father has given to him "Shall" come to him just as much as he believed everything else he said. He didn't say hopefully all the father gives him will come to him, or most of them would come to him, he said they would. It wasn't a matter of maybe. Understanding that the context of these verses is believing on Jesus, we can see that Jesus confidently believed that all that were his would believe on him, or in other words, all that the father has seen believing on him in the beginning would believe on him.

Jesus was speaking of the surety of salvation. The blessed assurance of faith. The knowing that one is absolutely and altogether saved through the finished work of the cross. Given the gift of right standing with God with a confidence that you'll never be defeated or separated from him. And a confidence that because Jesus took my punishment, I will not be judged like an unbeliever. Oh, praise the lord for his goodness friends, this is his plan and it's wonderful.

I want my people to know how saved they are and how pleased with them I am

In my discovery of this marvelous truth in the scriptures I asked the lord what is the purpose of this? Why are you allowing me to see this? His answer left me with a passion to preach the full accomplishment of Christ at calvary, the full finished work as its presented in scripture and a burden for all the sheep who don't know how much he loves them and what was accomplished at calvary for them, who live under condemnation.

He said to me, *"I want my people to know how saved they are and how pleased with them I am."*

I became intensely aware through a knowing within that his heart is so grieved because of shepherds that have beaten the sheep either knowingly or unknowingly, instead of feeding them. His heart hurts for all his children that have a wrong concept of him and don't know him as the love that he is. Oh, how he longs for them to see him as abba. It hurts his heart when his children walk around in condemnation with their heads down never experiencing the life he has for them and never coming into an awareness and an understanding of the great love that he has for them, and how valuable they are to him. Friend, God wants you to know that he is your Father that's interested in the affairs of your life.

I knew I had to compile a list of all the scriptures in the bible that speak on this matter and put them all into one piece of literature. I believe many people are going to be helped through the insight in this book. I love the book of 1st John. One of Johns main emphases was that believers may *"know that ye have eternal life."* I want to make a statement and I want you to hear me. It's possible for people that are born again to not know that they have eternal life, in fact, many Christians do not know how saved they are or how much of a full price was paid on their behalf. But by the grace of God that is going to change!

What did John mean by that statement, *"that ye may know that ye have eternal life?"* We understand that he was addressing the issue of false teachers in this epistle that had crept into the church that were bringing unsuspected believers back into bondage and as the apostle Paul stated in *Galatians 5:4 Christ is become of none effect unto you, you who are seeking to be justified by law; you have fallen from grace.* A main goal of the apostle John in his first epistle is to remove any doubt in the mind and heart of those that would read it who had placed faith in Christ, as to whether they were truly saved or not. False teachers were trying to convince converts that they also had to keep the law if they were to be saved and were through doing this overthrowing the faith of some. As we shall see, he repeatedly expresses his desire for believers to *know* they have eternal life. Or in other words, to be so certain, assured and confident that there is no way they could doubt it or ever have another fearful and dreadful thought of being rejected by the creator. He even goes as far as to say that God's perfect love casts out the fear of being rejected by him so that we may have boldness in the day of judgement.

1 John 4:17-18 KJV Herein is our love made perfect, that we may have boldness in the day of judgment: because as he is, so are we in this world. There is no fear in love; but perfect love casteth out fear: because fear hath torment. He that feareth is not made perfect in love.

1 John 4:17-18 NASB By this, love is perfected with us, so that we may have confidence in the day of judgment; because as He is, we also are in this world. There is no fear in love, but perfect love drives out fear, because fear involves punishment, and the one who fears is not perfected in love.

Notice that the kind of fear the perfect love of God should cast out of our lives is the fear that has to do with punishment or torment. This is actually a reference to the fear of being rejected by God our father on the day of judgment, or fear of condemnation in other words. An adequate understanding of God's perfect love for us will remove condemnation which is the fear of being rejected by him and going to hell.

John goes on to tell us that we may have boldness in the day of judgement. Boldness means confidence and absence of fear. Brothers and sisters, this is telling us we don't have to be afraid of being rejected on the day of judgment, but that we can be confident that we are his.

Also notice that the reason we can have this boldness or absence of fear on the day of judgment is because of something. He says it's *"because as he is – so are we in this world."*

What a statement! As he is. He is referring to God the father and Christ the son. As he is, so are we? What does this mean? We must ask how he is for us to know how we are. He is righteous among other things. And *"as he is, so are we"* righteous. But it doesn't stop there. He says we are as he is *"in this world"* or in this life right now. Wait a minute, you mean the bible says we are as God is right now in this world? According to the word of God, if you are born again, you are. This is obviously not referring to your flesh or your mind, will, or emotions. It's referring to your born-again spirit. The bible gives us two reasons we don't have to be afraid of being condemned or rejected by our father God. Number one – his perfect love drives out the fear of punishment. Number two – he has made us righteous "as he is." That's awesome!

There are thousands upon thousands of truly born-again Christians that do not possess a solid assurance of faith. They don't know that they are sealed unto the day of redemption and they have been given the gift of righteousness or right standing with God as Romans 5:17 puts it. And they don't know that they have been made the righteousness of God as 2 Corinthians 5:21 tells us we have been made. Gods word tells us to draw near with a true heart in *full assurance of faith* in Hebrews 10:22, full assurance that we have been redeemed in other words.

The assurance of Faith is the confidence that I'm his and he will never reject me

What is the assurance of faith? The assurance of faith is the confidence that he will never reject me or condemn me. It's being fully persuaded that there is nothing that can separate me from his love. I am locked into his love. The assurance of faith is one of the most precious things a believer can have. It's a vital piece of our Christian walk and yet many Christians do not possess an adequate security or confidence of being his. Friend, when you see things in their entirety, behold the bigger picture that is, it produces such a peace inside and a definite knowing of the hope of his calling.

1 John 1:2 KJV For the life was manifested, and we have seen it, and bear witness, and shew unto you that eternal life, which was with the father, and was manifested unto us.

1 John 1:4 KJV And these things write we unto you, that your joy may be full.

1 John 2:25 KJV And this is the promise that he hath promised us, even eternal life.

1 John 5:11 KJV And this is the record, that God hath given to us eternal life, and this life is in his son.

1 John 5:13 KJV These things have I written unto you that believe on the name of the son of God; that ye may know that ye have eternal life…

Considering the statements in the above scripture references "we bear witness and shew unto you eternal life", "these things we write unto you that your joy may be full", "this is the promise he hath made unto us even eternal life" and " these things have I written unto you that believe on the name of the son of god; that ye may know that ye have eternal life", we can readily see that God our father desires his children to know beyond a shadow of a doubt that they are totally and completely saved, that they are his through the finished work.

John 3:15 KJV That whosoever believeth in him should not perish but have eternal life.

John 17:2 KJV As thou hast given him power over all flesh, that he should give eternal life to as many as thou hast given him.

Acts 13:48 KJV And when the gentiles heard this, they were glad, and glorified the word of the lord: and as many as were ordained to eternal life believed.

Ordain [G5021 tasso; to assign, to arrange, to appoint]

It is my prayer that by this point you are beginning to see the depth of the love that God has for each of his children. And that you are beginning to understand the reality of the fact that because the price of the finished work that was paid on your behalf and because God knew ahead of time that you would be his and that you would be a believer, you have been completely justified and declared blameless by him. And as the scripture puts it in

Hebrews 10:14 KJV For by one offering he has forever perfected those who are sanctified.

CHAPTER 4

ONCE AND FOR ALL, SO WHO SHALL LAY ANYTHING?

Hebrews 10:14 KJV For by one offering he hath perfected forever them that are sanctified.

Romans 8:33 KJV Who shall lay anything to the charge of Gods elect? It is God that justifieth.

Who shall lay anything? Better yet, who can lay anything to the charge of Gods elect? What does that mean exactly? Let's break it down. The apostle Paul was emphasizing the power of the foreknowledge of God in the preceding verses and the depth of the justification that the believer has received due to what Jesus has done on their behalf. The blood of Christ speaks better things than that of Abel. Throughout the ages of eternity, the blood of Jesus Christ will speak on behalf of those that were foreknown by God.

Hebrews 9:12, KJV Neither by the blood of goats and calves, but by his own blood he entered in once into the holy place, having obtained eternal redemption for us.

He entered in once into the holy place, having obtained eternal redemption for us. Let's look at what these words used in Romans 8:33 mean in the Greek.

Vs. 33 *Who shall lay anything* [G1458 egkaleho; to come forward as an accuser, bring charge against, 2. To be accused, to lay to the charge, to place a debt upon]

to the charge (against) *Gods elect* [G1588 eklektos; picked out, chosen, elect]

Did you catch that? What he is asking is since God already knows all who will ever believe on Christ and already considers them his and to be in Christ, there is nothing they could ever do to escape the love he has for them and has surrounded them with. And if this be the case, then *"who shall lay anything"* or who is able in other words to lay anything upon the account of a believing one seeing that it was God that justified them because he knew them from the beginning? Who is able to make sin appear on the slate of a child of the all-knowing God? That is the true question. And I'll ask it like the apostle Paul, who is able to lay anything to the account of a picked out one? Who can cause God, who is love himself, to reject one of his fore known ones? I believe this is why he went on to say, who shall separate us from the love of God, because there is no person or thing or sin or failure or amount of fear that has the power to separate us from God and his love for us if we were truly known by him in the beginning. His love for us has gone before us.

The fact that there is no thing or person that can cause us to be separated from his love suggests to us again that it is not possible for a truly elect and foreknown one to ever be separated from God. Truly the question that was asked by the apostle Paul was a good one, *"what can we say to these things? If God be for us, who can be against us?"* The obvious answer to that is nobody. And the answer to the *question "who shall lay anything to the charge of Gods elect?"* is another resounding nobody!

"Is there unrighteousness with God" since he knows all things ahead of time? Is it unfair that he already knows the outcome of every single person even though they have a freewill? Was it unrighteous of God to have given us the power of choice when he knew what we would do with it? Of course not, or as Paul put it, *"God forbid."* Friends, it may seem unfair to some for God to give us a freewill knowing what we are going to do with it, but the apostle Paul addressed this issue and was letting us know that it's not an unrighteous or unfair thing for God to already know what every individual is going to do with the will that he gave them. After all he is God isn't he? Would you want to serve a God that doesn't know all things ahead of time? I don't think I would. There is no greater feeling than knowing that God already knows your outcome and it is good. I made that statement based on *Romans 8:28 We know that all things work together for good to them that love God, to them that are called according to his purpose.* All things must ultimately work out for your good. At some point, every single child of God arrives to what is good. Let's look at a few very powerful scriptures in Romans 9:

Romans 9:11-23 For the children being not yet born, neither having done any good or evil, that the purpose of God according to election might stand, not of works, but of him that calleth; It was said unto her, the elder shall serve the younger. As it is written, Jacob have I loved, but Esau have I hated. What shall we say to these things? Is there unrighteousness with God? God forbid. For he saith to Moses, I will have mercy on whom I will have mercy, and I will have compassion on whom I will have compassion. So then it is not of him that willeth, nor of him that runneth, but of God that sheweth mercy.

For the scripture saith unto pharaoh, Even for this same purpose have I raised thee up, that I might shew my power in thee, and that my name might be declared throughout all the earth. Therefore hath he mercy on whom he will have mercy, and whom he will he hardeneth. Thou wilt say to me, why doth he yet find fault? For who hath resisted his will? Nay but, O man, who art thou that repliest against God? Shall the thing formed say to him that formed it, why hast thou made me thus? Hath not the potter power over the clay, of the same lump to make one vessel unto honor, and another unto dishonor? What if God, willing to shew his wrath, and to make his power known, endured with much longsuffering the vessels of wrath fitted to destruction. And that he might make known the riches of his glory on the vessels of mercy, which he had afore prepared unto glory

I gave this chapter the title "once and for all, so who shall lay anything?" for a reason. And the reason is because I want people to understand something. The reason that we have eternal redemption is because God decided before he created the world that all who would ever accept the gift of salvation by putting their faith in Christ would be justified and blameless in his sight according to Ephesians 1:4-5. It lets us know he decided this before he made anything. That is why we have eternal life, because he already knew us in the beginning before he made anything, he knew we would be his and went ahead and considered us blameless in his sight.

That is the other side of eternal redemption, not the side of it that is ahead of us, but that which was before. He set it up that way, that us believing on Christ would please him so greatly that he would call innocent those who were not innocent and blameless those who were not blameless, simply because they believed that what he did for them was enough. Will you believe his report? Do you believe that what Jesus did for you in your place was enough? Or do you think you have to add to it? Do you think you are saved by your works? Or by Jesus perfect sacrifice? It truly is finished. Friend there's a reason the gospel is called good news.

The apostle Paul preached a message that included such a heavy emphasis on grace and predestination that some questioned what he was really saying and misunderstood the message to the extent that they said he was encouraging people to sin, which as you and I know, that isn't what he was doing. He was proclaiming the good news of the kingdom concerning election and grace and got accused of encouraging people to sin so that grace may abound. These accusations against the good news of God's grace still exist today yet in subtle form. Today the message of Gods unconditional love and grace toward his children is opposed not by sinners, but by the ones who are supposed to know what the scriptures teach on this subject. I have even heard it myself from the mouth of another minister who was opposing the message of God's grace that sounded almost identical to what the apostle Paul was accused of. Many legalistic preachers and religious folks in general have the idea that people are looking for a reason to get by with sin. Many have the kind of thinking where they think that unless God's people are afraid of being rejected by him and going to hell, they might run off and live in sin. And this is just not true, I know many people who know they are redeemed and have no fear of going to hell if they make a mistake and they live more godly lives than some religious Christians I've seen, and they are not self-righteous. Some think if you preach grace too strong, people will just use it as an excuse to sin. Understand this is not the case for most. It is true that some have taken the message of grace and used it improperly to justify a lifestyle of sloppy living. But that doesn't change what the word of God teaches us, nor should it produce reluctancy with preaching the subject of grace. There are always going to be people who don't understand the message and use it to justify ungodly character, but they are a small percentage. And there are always going to be people who misunderstand the message and think that you are saying there are no consequences for sinful living, but that didn't change the message that the apostle Paul preached. He still preached it despite the few that misunderstood what he was actually saying, and we should too.

Some ministers are so scared that if you tell people how big the grace of God is for his children that they will run off and live in sin. What ministers must understand is that the true sheep don't want to sin and get by with it. The true sheep are not looking for a free pass to sin. Most believers are not just looking towards the next wrong thing they can do and hopefully not get caught. The truth is that most people would want out of sin if they knew there was a way out. I want every minister of the gospel that reads this to understand that God has called us to feed the sheep not beat the sheep. Jesus had a different concept than people that think if you believe too much in the grace of God and his promise that there's no condemnation to you that you will use it as a license to sin. Jesus believed the contrary, he believed that the greater you are aware of how forgiven you are, the more you will love him, as he expressed in Luke 7:47.

If a person ever truly discovers how much love God the Father and the Lord Jesus have for them and how forgiven they really are, they will be set free from condemnation forever and not only that, but they will also reap massive benefit from possessing an adequate understanding in this area, and sin will not have dominion over them because they will come out from under law and begin living under grace. Jesus really believed that the more you are aware, or the greater you know beyond doubt that you are completely forgiven and are his, the more you will love him. It is something that comes naturally. The carnal mind cannot wrap itself around this concept, it takes the spirit of God opening the eyes of a person. If you know how much you are loved by him, you will love him more than the rest, ask John he knows. We will explore in the next chapter the difference between how God dealt with his people under the old covenant and how he deals with his children in the new and better covenant. This new and living covenant we are in now is better than the last one and has better promises too.

1 Corinthians 3:15 KJV If any man's work shall be burned, he shall suffer loss: but he himself shall be saved; yet so as by fire.

In this scripture the apostle Paul was speaking of an individual being able to lose their reward, or in other words to live an unrewardable life, yet the individual will still be saved as we see in the statement *"but he himself shall be saved."* He was making it clear that a person is capable of not doing a rewardable work or living a rewardable life necessarily, but that person will still be saved if he has been born again. The purpose us seeing this is that you might finally get free from condemnation and receive grace so you can begin to live as the more than conqueror you really are.

Chapter 5

This is as the waters of Noah to me

Isaiah 54:8-10 KJV In a little wrath I hid my face from the for a moment; but with everlasting kindness will I have mercy on thee, saith the Lord thy redeemer. For this is as the waters of Noah unto me: for as I have sworn that the waters of Noah should no more go over the earth; so have I sworn that I would not be wroth with thee, nor rebuke thee. For the mountains shall depart, and the hills be removed; but my kindness shall not depart from thee, neither shall the covenant of my peace be removed, saith the Lord that hath mercy on thee.

I love the way the passion translation puts it.

Isaiah 54:8-10 TPT In a surge of anger, for just the briefest moment, I hid my face from you, but with everlasting kindness, I will show you my cherishing love, says Yahweh, your kinsman-redeemer. To me, this is like the time when I vowed that the waters of Noah's flood would never again cover the earth. Now I vow to you that I will never be angry with you nor rebuke you. Even if the mountains were to crumble and the hills disappear, my heart of steadfast love will never leave you, and my covenant of peace with you will never be shaken, says Yahweh, whose love and compassion will never give up on you.

Because what was finished by Jesus at the cross was so great God has vowed to all his children that he will never be angry with them or rebuke them. This was originally written to Israel, but as we shall see, it was written prophetically to the church.

Most students of the word are already aware that this chapter in Isaiah speaks of the transition from how God dealt with his servants under the old covenant who viewed right standing with him as something that must be earned and how he would deal with the New Testament believer who simply accepts righteousness as a gift. We see that God reveals himself as *"The Lord your redeemer"* in these passages of scripture and this has a twofold meaning behind it and is referring to not only Israel but those who would be the seed of Abraham under the new covenant. That being said, we can't say that this only applies to the nation of Israel and not to us in the new covenant because the word of God tells us the covenant we're under now is a better covenant established upon better promises in Hebrews 8:6. Now that we have established that these verses are for us we are ready to dive into it. Let's look and see what God is trying to relate to us.

He emphasizes the love he has for us through a couple of statements that we'll look at. He also made it clear that he would never be angry with one of his redeemed ones and that his kindness would not depart from them, and the covenant of his peace would not be removed. This must be speaking us in the new covenant friends because God's wrath could come upon those under the old covenant and his kindness could depart from them. But it's not the case for the one who Jesus hung on the tree in place of. Again, we can see that he is speaking to New Testament believers because he reveals himself as *"the lord your redeemer"*, redemption was not available until the new covenant came.

He speaks of how he had hidden his face for a brief moment in wrath and then goes on to say *"but with everlasting kindness will I have mercy on you says the lord thy redeemer."* He is contrasting his wrath with his kindness and expresses how excited he is to treat his children this way. He also says that those that know him as *"redeemer"* would never again see his wrath.

We can clearly see this in the statement, *"but with everlasting kindness will I have mercy on you."* He indicated that his wrath was but for a moment and that his kindness would be *"everlasting."* His delight to show kindness to his redeemed is greater than they can imagine.

What is everlasting kindness?

everlasting- H5769 olam olam; long duration, antiquity, for ever, everlasting, evermore, perpetual, old, ancient, always *kindness-* H2617 chesed; goodness, kindness, faithfulness, beauty, favor, good deed, merciful

As we can readily see, God has made it clear that there would come a time that he would relate to and treat the individuals he was speaking of, in an entirely different way than he had in the past. In the past he had dealt with his servants in anger and judgement, but once this time of the new and living covenant comes, all sin for his children would be judged at the cross and he would deal with them in unconditional love and grace on a constant basis. He made it clear that this new way that he would relate and deal with his people under the new covenant would be completely different than that under the old through the statement, *"In a little wrath I hid my face from the for a moment; but with everlasting kindness will I have mercy on thee, saith the Lord thy redeemer."* This is wonderful news, but it gets better.

Verse *9 For this is as the waters of Noah unto me: for as I have sworn that the waters of Noah should no more go over the earth; so have I sworn that I would not be wroth with thee, nor rebuke thee.*

In order for us to understand the depth of what he is saying, it is important that we see that the *"this"* in verse 9 is the *"everlasting kindness"* he had spoken of in the preceding verse.

An oath without condition

This everlasting kindness, this perpetual favor I will show to you is as the waters of Noah to me. How is it as the waters of Noah to God? In Genesis chapter 9

God swore with an oath that he would never flood the earth again under any circumstances. But it wasn't just any oath, it was an oath without conditions. Normally an oath has conditions, but this one didn't. In other words, "No matter what, I will never ever flood the entire earth again!"

So when he says in Isaiah 54:9 *"As I swore that the waters of Noah should no more go over the earth, So have I sworn that I would not be angry with you nor rebuke you"* the *statements "As I swore"* along with *"So have I sworn"* make it obvious that he wanted the hearer to know that this oath to not ever be angry with them or rebuke them is also without condition as the oath to never flood the earth again was without condition. As I have sworn, so have I sworn or in the same manner have I sworn. This is remarkable. *"So have I sworn"* but how did he swear? He just simply said it would never happen again. And he wants his children to know that *"as I have sworn then without condition, so have I sworn regarding never being angry with you and my kindness never leaving you."*

I think we need to meditate on this. *"So have I sworn that I would not be angry with you nor rebuke you. For the mountains shall depart, and the hills be removed; but my kindness shall not depart from thee, neither shall the covenant of my peace be removed, saith the lord that hath mercy on thee."*

And as it is so beautifully put in the passion translation, *"Even if the mountains were to crumble and the hills disappear, my heart of steadfast, faithful love will never leave you, and my covenant of peace with you will not be shaken."*

He basically says the mountains and hills would disappear before this covenant could be broken. That is powerful my friend and we ought not overlook it. In the last verse of the chapter, verse 17 God said that the righteousness they would possess was from him and not their efforts through the statement *"and their righteousness is of me"* he wanted them to know that their right standing with him was *of* or from him and not themselves.

He goes on to say they would be established in righteousness or right standing with him in verse 14 *"In righteousness shalt thou be established."* I want to ask you a question…

What does it mean to be established in righteousness?

The answer will depend upon a person's concept of what righteousness is. I like this simple explanation and it is that righteousness is right standing with God and holiness on the other hand is the outward expression of the righteousness one has been made. Many people have confused and mixed the two, nonetheless righteousness is right standing with God. How do you become *"established"* in righteousness? Is that something you obtain through pursuit? No. A hundred times no! Friend, you don't become established in right standing with God over time. It's something that happens instantaneously. The moment you became born again you were declared the righteousness of God. The moment you became born again you were made the righteousness of God in Christ. *2 Corinthians 5:21 For he hath made him to be sin for us, who knew no sin; that we might be made the righteousness of God in him.* When you are made righteous you didn't earn it. When you are made righteous you didn't deserve it. When you are made righteous you are established in it at the very same time. You don't get made the righteousness of God and become established in it over time, you're established in right standing with God from that point on because he *made* you that way. He didn't just give us righteousness; he actually made us his righteousness. That's awesome. If God made us righteous, who are we to think we can make ourselves righteous. It is pride for a believer to think they have the ability to affect the righteous status that was given to them by God and that they have been made.

Who do you think you are?

I remember one occasion that took place a couple of years ago. I had made a mistake and my conscious was condemning me. I didn't know it was my conscience at the time and felt condemned and as if I could never be accepted by God. And I remember in the middle of my shame, guilt, and feelings of condemnation I heard the lord say to me, *"Who do you think you are?"* When I heard this, I wondered what it could mean and then he continued, *"Who do you think you are thinking you have the power to change my mind?"* In that moment I knew what he was saying. He was referring to how I had been condemning myself thinking it was him condemning me, and that he hadn't changed his mind about having made me righteous. He was reminding me that there was no condemnation to them who are in Christ Jesus. He reminded me that I didn't have the power to change his mind, for he had chosen me in Christ before the foundation of the world and declared me blameless so who was I to think I was condemned. His love for me had already seen and factored into the equation any failure or mistake I may ever have. He knew every time I would miss it before he saved me and yet he still chose to, better yet he knew the failures and mistakes of all his children before they got here. Did you get that? God already knows every choice we will make before he made anything, so we don't have to feel as if he was surprised by it because he wasn't. Is this an encouragement to sin? NO, of course not. But its sometimes necessary to put a disclaimer out there when going in depth speaking of grace, predestination and election because the message is difficult for the carnal mind to grasp. And some people just can't comprehend a God that wants to be good to his children and not judge them with the world. Some may find it difficult to believe that God could be that good, but it doesn't change the fact that he is.

CHAPTER 6

FOREKNOWN AND LOVED BEFOREHAND

I remember the cloud like it was yesterday

I remember that night like it was yesterday, back in 2016… when the cloud descended from the top of my room and overshadowed me. It wasn't a visible cloud as I had seen as a young boy. I couldn't see it, but I knew it was there. I could feel it all over me and with it came this intense knowing that I was loved before I got here. I became intensely aware of my father's love that existed for me before the world was made. This was the love of my father who knew me from the beginning. He was making himself real to me. I was aware of my sin, and my face was covered with shame. I remember covering my face because of not feeling worthy to be loved like this. Tears rolled down my cheeks as I melted in this extravagant love that enveloped me. I was his. I knew I was his. I knew nothing could ever separate me from him because his love for me existed before the world was made. I knew that even though I was struggling in my personal life at that time he still loved me the same and I hadn't been separated from him as I thought I had. It was as if he couldn't even see any of the flaws I could see and only knew how to see me one way and that was as his beloved. I was aware that there was nothing that I could do to separate me from this eternal love for me that has always existed in his heart.

God's love toward you had no beginning

I want to ask a few questions to get you thinking. We all agree that the love of God for his children never ceases or comes to an end. But has it ever crossed our minds that not only does the love of God for us not have an end, it also had no beginning. The eternal love of God for us had no beginning. It is without beginning or end. Friend, God did not start loving you when you grew in character and self-improved. He did not start loving you once you were lovable. He didn't start loving you when you were born. One may argue that the love of God for an individual begins at the point of conception. And while this an attempt to understand his love, this view is limited. His love for you has existed inside of him all along. For as far back in time as you can go that God himself existed, and we know he always has, the love that he is and has for his children existed too. That is awesome!

I gave this chapter the title I gave it because I believe it will help people to understand the eternal nature of the love of God. God's love has always existed as long as he has, because he is love.

How did he foreknow us?

If you are born again or ever become a believer at any point in your life and accept the gift of salvation, that means he knew you before you got here. But he didn't know you in any kind of way. The way he knew his children before he made anything is with an unconditional love and an abundance of grace. Plenty enough of an abundance to get you through life. Plenty enough love to permanently eradicate fear and produce great confidence in him. He has known us intimately all along. God has ordained before the foundation of the world that all those that would ever be his would have his love shed abroad in their hearts by the Holy ghost which is given to them. He has also ordained that they would love him and others with the supply of the love that he gave them. He has also ordained that all things would work together for good for those individuals that are called, which he foresaw loving him and believing on Jesus.

If we examine a few verses of scripture in Romans chapter 8, we can see that the apostle Paul directly connected the inseparable love of God with his foreknowledge of us. He gives a discourse on how those that he foreknew he also predestinated and those he predestinated he also justified and those he justified he also glorified. It's interesting that all these things are written in the past tense. This was done purposely to emphasize the reality that its already done as far as God is concerned.

"Who shall lay anything to the charge of Gods elect?" and *"Who is he that condemneth?"*

These statements reveal something to us. He goes on to say, *"who shall separate us from the love of Christ?"* and gives a list of things that don't have the ability to separate us from the love that knew us all along. He says, *"who shall lay anything to the charge of God's elect?"* and goes on to say, *"who is he that condemneth?"* It was a rhetorical question, and the obvious answer is nobody. No thing or person has the ability to lay anything to our charge and therefore cause us to be condemned before God. And nothing has the power to separate us from the love of God which is in Christ Jesus now and was in him before the world was made.

The apostle Paul knew when he asked those questions what the answer was. He was using questions to prove his point. The word of God is showing us that the reason nothing can separate us from the love of God is because of this great foreknowledge of his. This is why the three questions can be found together *"who shall lay anything to the charge of God's elect?" "who is he that condemneth?"* and *"who shall separate us from the love of Christ?"* It can therefore be concluded that due to what was done for us at calvary, one of the reasons we can never be separated from the love of God is because it's not possible for anything to be laid upon the charge of God's elect. That my brothers and sisters is why he asked those questions. He was establishing that we are established right standing with God as Isaiah prophesied we would be. We are locked into the eternal love of God.

It might help us to hear it this way. Who has the power to place unforgiven sin on the slate of a redeemed child of God, seeing it was Christ that died and justified them? So who can condemn? And who has the power to separate us from the unconditional love of Christ and of God our father that existed for us before the world began?

Has it ever dawned on you that condemnation is a form of fear? Have you ever wondered what exactly is condemnation anyway? After all, it's our conscience that condemns us not God. Our physical carnal mind. It condemns us when we miss it, we feel guilty and ashamed. Our conscience goes to condemning us and produces these feelings of unworthiness, inadequacy and rejection. The goal of condemnation is to make us feel and believe that we have been rejected by our father so we will live defeated. I believe the reason is because we naturally won't approach our dad if we believe that he's mad at us or if we believe he has condemned us. Please understand that it is not your father that is condemning you if you have been born again. Be free as you receive the word. Condemnation is the fear of being rejected by God and it's often accompanied by the fear of going to hell also. But when you come in contact with the truth, proper knowledge of the love of God will set you free from the fear of being rejected by him. When truth comes, lies must get out. Friend, there is absolutely no condemnation to those who are in Christ Jesus. This is the true gospel of the finished work of Christ. Jesus through his own blood has paid it all. He has bore your sins. He has carried your sorrows, he himself took your infirmities and with his stripes you are healed. He has absorbed into his beaten, broken and bruised body that hung on the tree in your place all the holy and righteous judgment of God that you would ever deserve. Let the spirit reveal to you how redeemed you are. Let the word of God determine what you believe, not maw-maw or the preacher. When you fully embrace his love for you, the fear and condemnation you have carried for years will melt off like butter and you will have confidence that you are saved and even boldness on the day of judgement.

Isn't the day of judgement a fearful day?

But shouldn't the day of judgement be a fearful day? Yes, for the one who never believed on Jesus and accepted the free gift of salvation during their life on earth. But for the believing ones, we will not be judged with the world. Ours is a completely different judgment. We will be before the judgment seat of Christ, or the mercy seat in other words. And the ones who never accepted Jesus will be judged at the great white throne judgment by God the father. That day will be a dreadful day for those individuals. But for you and I, it will be a glorious celebration and receiving of gifts. This is one of the reasons why the apostle John said in *1 John 4:17 Herein is our love made perfect, that we may have boldness in the day of judgement...*

For the first few years of my Christian journey, I attended churches that were very critical and condemning. I became very legalistic and critical of others through the culture I was exposed to. I remember inviting my mother to church but telling her she couldn't wear any jewelry and she had to wear a dress. During these few years, I was never taught to know God as my father. I wasn't taught who I am in Christ. I wasn't taught the tremendous love he has for me and that he has made me his righteousness and set me completely free from the law of sin and of death. I wasn't taught the authority I have over the devil. I wasn't taught that it was God's will for me to prosper and be in health. I wasn't taught what faith is and how to release my faith to see the promises of God manifest in my life, on the contrary I was taught to beg and plead with God to give me things that were already granted. Any kind of teaching on faith or grace or how to prosper was considered by the church culture to be false. I wasn't taught about grace. I wasn't taught that I continue in the lord receiving grace just as I did when I first accepted his salvation. And the main thing I wasn't taught was the love of God.

You're probably thinking, "what were you taught then?" I was taught how to be critical of others. I was taught how to take scriptures out of context. I was taught how to walk in constant unworthiness and fear of being rejected by God and sentenced to eternity in hell. I was taught it was a sin to wear jewelry. I was taught it was sin to own a television or go to the movies. I wasn't taught that the reason the Holy spirit comes in is to clean us up, rather I was told that he wouldn't come in until I cleaned myself up. I was taught a version of God that caused me to fear him in an unhealthy way. I was taught a God that was angry and ready to judge me at all times. I understand now that the reason people are so ready to condemn is because that's how they think God is dealing with them. I was taught to be sin conscious instead of righteousness conscious.

I spent years of my life under the wrong kind of culture. By that I mean I was constantly aware that I was unworthy of anything from him and that he was displeased with me and that he may cause unfortunate circumstances to come my way if I mess up and there was no way for me to know that I had eternal life and was on my way to heaven. The churches I attended lived in a bubble and their view of the world was that all other churches were deceived and if they didn't believe exactly as they did on every subject, they wouldn't associate with them. I understand they had good intentions and that the things we experience contribute to our growth. I learned a lot of things I would not have learned otherwise so I am thankful for the experience. However, I am glad those days are over and revelation knowledge of the word of God has come.

I now understand that the devil loves it when believers don't know they are truly saved. He loves to see truly born-again believers walking in condemnation, guilt and shame. Not understanding the fundamental things such as the love of God can completely rob a person of the joy of salvation and the freedom of the spirit. There are of course other subjects in scripture that are foundational for reigning in life and living in victory. The love of God is the basis of everything. When a believer begins to understand certain things, especially the Love God has for them, and that he has made them righteous, they will begin to live without fear.

CHAPTER 7

HE THAT IS FORGIVEN MUCH, LOVES MUCH

Luke 7:47 KJV Wherefore I say unto thee, her sins, which are many, are forgiven; for she loved much: but to whom little is forgiven, the same loveth little.

Luke 7:47 TPT She has been forgiven of all her many sins. This is why she has shown me such extravagant love. But those who assume they have very little to be forgiven will love me very little.

As I meditated on this scripture, I knew that it deserved a chapter for itself. One of the pharisees had desired Jesus to eat with him and he went. While he was there a woman in the city found out he was eating at the pharisees house and brought an alabaster box of ointment. She began to wash Jesus feet with her tears and wipe them with her hair and anointed them with the ointment. When the pharisee saw this, he said within, *"if this man were truly a prophet, he would have known what kind of woman that is touching him, she's a sinner."* Jesus knew what he was thinking and proceeded to tell him a parable.

Luke 7:40-47 KJV And Jesus answering said unto him, Simon, I have somewhat to say unto thee. And he saith, Master, say on. There was a certain creditor which had two debtors: the one owed five hundred pence, and the other fifty. And when they had nothing to pay, he frankly forgave them both. Tell me therefore, which of them will love him most? Simon answered and said, I suppose that he, to whom he forgave most. And he said unto him, Thou hast rightly judged. And he turned to the woman, and said unto Simon, Seest thou this woman? I entered into thine house, thou gavest me no water for my feet: but she hath washed my feet with tears, and wiped them with the hairs of her head. Thou gavest me no kiss: but this woman since the time I came in hath not ceased to kiss my feet. My head with oil thou didst not anoint: but this woman hath anointed my feet with ointment. Wherefore I say unto thee, Her sins, which are many, are forgiven; for she loved much: but to whom little is forgiven, the same loveth little.

The NASB puts it like this:

And Jesus responded and said to him, "Simon, I have something to say to you." And he replied, "Say it, Teacher." "A moneylender had two debtors: the one owed five hundred denarii, and the other, fifty. When they were unable to repay, he canceled the debts of both. So which of them will love him more?" Simon answered and said, "I assume the one for whom he canceled the greater debt." And He said to him, "You have judged correctly." And turning toward the woman, He said to Simon, "Do you see this woman? I entered your house; you gave Me no water for My feet, but she has wet My feet with her tears and wiped them with her hair. You gave Me no kiss; but she has not stopped kissing My feet since the time I came in. You did not anoint My head with oil, but she anointed My feet with perfume. For this reason I say to you, her sins, which are many, have been forgiven, for she loved much; but the one who is forgiven little, loves little."

Jesus showed this pharisee through the parable why the woman loved him so much. He used debt to explain why. If you have ever dealt with debt or seen someone that has, you know how much it can affect their lives and even their health if they let it. I want you to think about that. The debt owed by these two individuals was vastly different. And the one with the greater debt lived his life wondering how he would pay it back because of the great size of the debt. If we can see an accurate picture of how great a debt was owed on our part that was paid by Jesus, we will be filled with gratitude and love for him. We owed a debt we could not pay. He paid a debt he did not owe. Think about how robbed of joy or hope that individual who owed the very large debt was compared to the one who owed a small debt. It makes perfect sense that this one would express greater gratitude because of the perceived value of the amount of debt that was forgiven.

Naturally, a person with a hundred thousand- or million-dollar debt would be more thankful than a person with a thousand- or ten-thousand-dollar debt if the debt was cancelled. Why? Because a million dollars carries a greater value than a thousand dollars. The debt that we owed was far greater than anything we could ever pay. And the price that Jesus paid on our behalf was far greater than any number of mistakes we could have in life. That is the great exchange.

Let's take a look at the statement Jesus made in the above text - *"which of the two debtors would be most thankful?"*

Simon responded by saying, *"the one who had the greater debt."* Jesus responds and tells him that he had judged rightly.

The love, adoration, thanksgiving and praise that an individual expresses towards their heavenly father and the lord Jesus will be greatly affected by how they feel he thinks of them and how well the redemption they have received has been taught to them, those two things. How they think God is dealing with them and how well they understand how much forgiveness they have been given. How well they understand that their right standing with the father is a gift and that it is a finished work. He entered in once and obtained for us eternal redemption. What he did with his own blood was more than enough. The power of grace begins to rule in our life when we see how forgiven and accepted we truly are by our father and by the Lord Jesus, and our love for them flourishes. We just examined the statement Jesus made. He made it clear that those who are aware that they are forgiven of much will love him much. He set it up that way. Pastors and leaders, the way to get the sheep to draw near to the lord is by revealing to them how much he loves them and how he loves to spend time with them and hear their prayers. If you can impart to them a shift in the way they relate to their father and reveal to them how he desires them to truly know him, they will run to him and love righteousness, holiness, and godly living. It isn't the number of sins that determines how great of a debt a person owes, and needs pardoned for. Rather, it's the inherent fallen state that indwells every human being at the time of birth. That being born into sin is where the weight of the debt lies. Essentially, all people were born with the same sin debt. Likewise, the price that was paid for the elect was equally an overpayment for all of them. The blood of Jesus is more powerful than any amount of sin. This is not an encouragement to sin, but a stripping of its power to rule us and dominate in our lives, for he has condemned sin in the flesh. For the power of sin has always been and will always lie in condemnation that comes from the law of sin in our members. And if condemnation can be eradicated from a believer's life, the power that sin appears to have over them will give way to the spirit of life that has already made them free in Christ. It is possible to live a fear free life, in righteousness consciousness.

Although our conscious is a good compass to show us if we've missed the mark, it's still a flawed system because all it knows to do is give us shame, guilt, and feelings of condemnation and unworthiness which are essential elements in perpetuating the cycle of sin. This is why the word of God taught us in Romans chapter 7 and 8 that the solution to being dominated and overcome by the flesh is through getting under a greater law, the law of the spirit of life in Christ Jesus which requires the removal of condemnation and believing one is dead to sin and alive unto God to get under. The inner witness is how the new covenant believer is to be lead. Where I missed it for years in my life was confusing my conscience with God. And this is something I think many believers go through because of the kind of preaching and teaching they sit under and the lack of proper teaching. I lived under condemnation for years. The entire time it was my conscious that was condemning me not God, but I thought it was him. The truth is that our conscious can't stop condemning us fully and completely until we know that our father hasn't condemned us and has justified us and declared us innocent in his sight. It's then we can begin to see ourselves that way and see ourselves as who he says we are, and our behavior and habits that need changing will follow. It is vital for believers to be taught a proper concept of God as a loving father, and to be taught who they are now that they are a new creature in Christ Jesus, because until the mind is renewed to think in line with who the law of the spirit of life says we are, it will continue to think the way it always has. The word of God tells us to be transformed by the renewing or the renovating of our thinking because transformation cannot come in the capacity it needs to come until we do.

"We have to know how God see's us so we will know how to see ourselves"

We have to know how God sees us so we will know how to view ourselves. Great things are coming for those that know him. I like what John said in 1 John chapter 3. He said that when Jesus appears we shall be like him *"because we shall see him as he is."*

1 John 3:2 KJV Beloved, now are we the sons of God, and it doth not yet appear what we shall be: but we know that, when he shall appear, we shall be like him; for we shall see him as he is.

I understand that this is a clear reference to Christ's return. But if we can benefit from seeing him as he is right now, we should want that also.

How is He? And is it possible to see him as he is in this present moment and be like him?

First let's address the first question. How is He? In chapter 4 of the same epistle the word of God says in both verses 8 and 16 that *"God is Love."* This double mention of the statement indicates to us a strong emphasis of this fact. He wanted his readers to undoubtedly believe and know that God their father *is love.* This is how he desires to be known by you son or daughter of God. That he cares about the smallest details and deepest desires of your heart. In Jeremiah 33:8-9 God said he would cleanse their iniquity and it would be a name of joy and praise unto him. In these two verses of scripture, he reveals that he delights to forgive, it's his good pleasure. He says that his forgiveness would be a name of joy and a praise unto him and that all the nations would fear and tremble for all the goodness and prosperity that he gives. This is how he wants to be known by his children. God looked forward to the day that Jesus would come so that he would be able to treat his children as if they never sinned, that's why it pleased him to bruise him. The only thing we can't see about him now is the physical glorified aspect of things. That is the only thing of him we can't yet see. But who he is, we can see. We can see who he is from the pages of scripture. We can see him as the love that he is right now while we live on the earth. We don't have to live with a veil over our eyes that blocks us from ever seeing him in his fullness. The love of God is what our father is made of. He bleeds it through the pages of the bible. Jesus knew that believers will be like him when they see him as he is and for who he is and that's why it tells us *"we shall be like him, for we shall see him as he is."* That's awesome! Yes, it is possible to be like him right now in this present world by beholding and seeing him *"as he is"* and that is love. The greater understanding we possess of the love of God for us and how much we are truly forgiven, the greater we will love him.

.